My First Book of Earth

ALL ABOUT OUR PLANET FOR KIDS

STEPHANIE MANKA SCHUTTLER, PhD

ROCKRIDGE
PRESS

Dedicated to our beautiful planet Earth
that inspires me with wonder
and leaves me breathless in awe every day.

First Rockridge Press edition 2022

For general information on our other products and services, please contact our Customer Care Department within the United States at (866) 744-2665, or outside the United States at (510) 253-0500.

Hardcover ISBN: 978-1-68539-652-7
Paperback ISBN: 978-1-68539-199-7
eBook ISBN: 978-1-68539-989-4

Manufactured in the United States of America

Series Designer: Sean Doyle
Interior and Cover Designer: Michael Cook
Art Producer: Samantha Ulban
Editor: Laura Bryn Sisson
Production Editor: Ruth Sakata Corley
Production Manager: Lanore Coloprisco

All images used under license from Science Source, Shutterstock & iStock. Author photo courtesy of Stephanie Schuttler

10 9 8 7 6 5 4 3 2 1 0

Printed in China

This Book Belongs to:

Welcome to planet Earth!

Have you ever gone outside and . . . felt the dirt beneath your feet? Breathed in the fresh air? Or looked up at fluffy **clouds** in the sky? These things and more make up our amazing planet Earth!

Planets are large objects that move around the sun. There are eight planets in our **solar system**: Mercury, Venus, Earth, Mars, Jupiter, Saturn, Uranus, and Neptune.

Earth is special. It is the only known planet with living things like you and me.

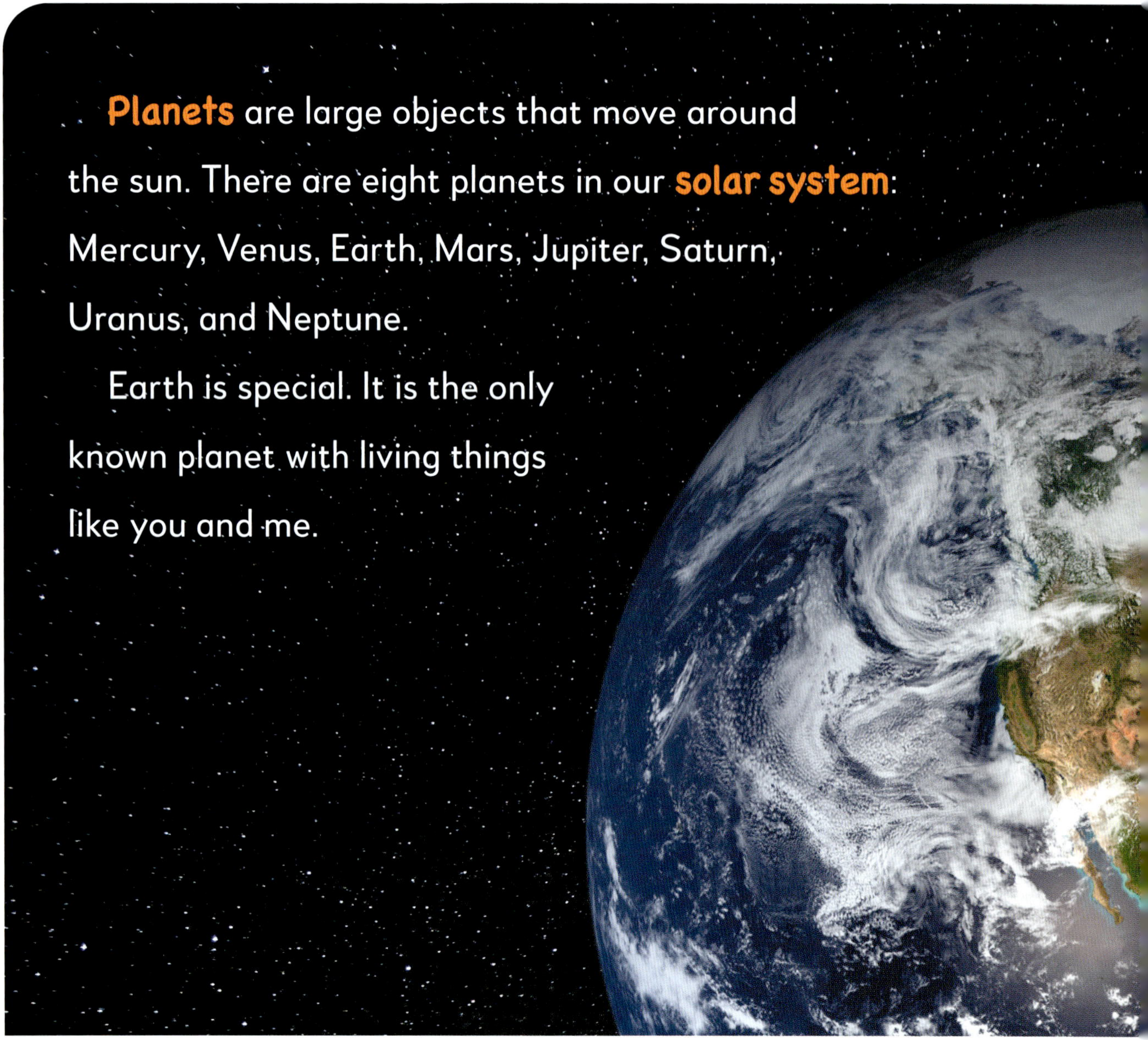

Earth is the third planet from the sun. It is neither too hot nor too cold. It has land and water, like oceans, lakes, and rain.

Earth is 4.5 billion years old. It is older than before any human lived. It is even older than the dinosaurs!

Inside the Earth

Earth is made up of different layers, like an onion.

At the center of Earth is the **inner core**. It is mostly made of **solid** iron and nickel.

The **outer core** layer surrounds the inner core. It is made of iron and nickel, too, but it is **liquid**.

Liquid flows freely and takes the shape of the container it is in. A solid holds its shape.

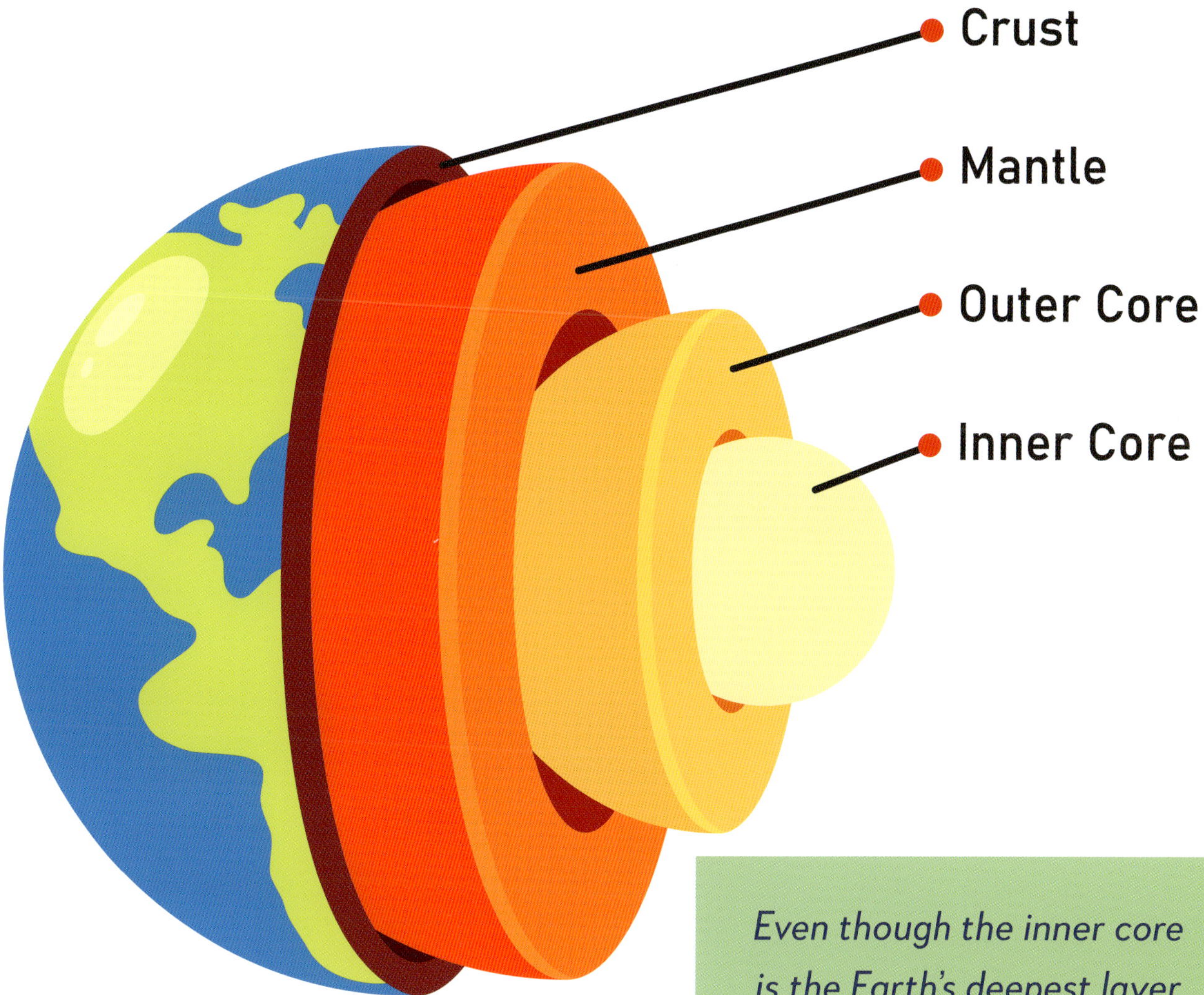

Even though the inner core is the Earth's deepest layer underground, it is as hot as the surface of the sun!

The next layer of Earth is the **mantle**. The mantle is mostly solid rock. It is very heavy. It contains more than half of the Earth's weight!

The top layer is the **crust**. It is the outside of Earth and the part we can see and touch. It is the Earth's smallest layer and is made of rock.

The Earth's Surface

Most of the Earth's crust is covered by water. The parts of the Earth's crust that are above water are called land.

Land has many different shapes and forms. Land can be tall like a mountain, or deep like a canyon. Land can be rough, rocky, smooth, or flat.

Did you know that mountains are not only found on land? The ocean has mountains, too. Scientists have found mountain ranges on the bottom of the ocean.

People live on land, but most of the Earth's surface is water. Earth is the only known planet that has lakes, rivers, and oceans.

There is so much water on Earth that it is sometimes called the "Blue Planet." When astronauts see Earth from space, it looks very blue.

Land

Less than half of the Earth's crust is land. The large areas of land separated by oceans are called continents.

Earth has seven continents: Africa, Asia, North America, South America, Australia, Europe, and Antarctica. Europe and Asia are connected and called Eurasia.

A long time ago, the continents made up one large land mass. Over time, the seven continents moved to where they are today.

Plates are large pieces of the Earth's crust. Hot liquid rock flows under the plates.

Continents are formed by **plate tectonics**. Over time, the plates move very slowly. When two plates push into each other, land can pile up and form mountains. When plates move away from each other, the mantle underneath is pushed up to form new crust.

Volcanoes

Volcanoes can look like mountains, but they are a very different type of landform. Volcanoes are openings in the Earth's crust where hot liquid rock, small solid rocks, and steam come out. Steam is water in a **gas** form. Over time, the liquid rock cools and can form a cone.

Volcanoes can also look like holes or cracks in the Earth's crust. Some are even underwater.

When the hot liquid rock is inside a volcano, it is called **magma***. After it comes out, it is called* **lava***.*

Trees and Plants

Plants are living things. They cover most of the Earth's land. Plants are in the ocean, too.

Plants are very important to us. They give us materials to make things like paper, clothes, and our homes. They give us food.

Can you name some of the plants you eat?

Plants also give us oxygen, a gas our body needs. Plants use sunlight and another gas called carbon dioxide to make their food. From this, they release oxygen. This is called **photosynthesis**.

Some places have many plants growing close together. Rain forests have so many trees that the leaves block sunlight from reaching the ground. In meadows, it can be hard to see the soil between all the grasses and flowers.

The tallest tree in the world is the redwood tree. The tallest redwood is almost as tall as 19 houses stacked on top of one another!

There is more freshwater underground, beneath the Earth's surface, than there is in all the rivers, streams, and lakes on top.

Water

More than half of the Earth's surface is water. All living things, like plants, animals, and people, need water to survive.

There are different types of water. **Freshwater** is found in lakes, rivers, streams, ponds, and wetlands. It is even found underground! Freshwater is the kind of water we drink.

Most freshwater is in the form of ice. Large amounts of ice are found at the top and bottom of the Earth where it is very cold.

The other type of water is **saltwater**. It gets its name because it contains a lot of salt. Saltwater is found mostly in oceans. Freshwater also has salt, but saltwater contains a lot more.

Oceans

Oceans cover more than half of the Earth. Almost all of the Earth's water is in oceans.

The oceans are all connected, but they are divided into five separate bodies of water. They are the Arctic, Atlantic, Indian, Pacific, and Southern oceans.

The oceans are very important to us. They store heat from the sun and move it around the planet, keeping it warm.

Oceans give us oxygen. Tiny plants in the ocean give us more than half of the oxygen we breathe.

We also get food from the oceans. Many animals call the ocean their home.

There is still so much to learn about the oceans. We know more about the surface of the **moon** than we do about the bottom of the ocean!

The largest animal ever to live on Earth is the blue whale. It lives in the ocean and is bigger than any dinosaur.

The Atmosphere

All around Earth is a layer of gases we can't see called the **atmosphere**. A gas is something with no shape that will fill a container.

One gas in the atmosphere is the oxygen we get from plants. Another gas is nitrogen. Nitrogen makes up the largest part of the atmosphere.

The Earth's atmosphere starts at the ground and goes up into outer space. It has five main layers: the troposphere, stratosphere, mesosphere, thermosphere, and exosphere. The layer closest to Earth is the troposphere.

Scientists aren't sure where the Earth's atmosphere ends and where outer space begins! There is no clear border.

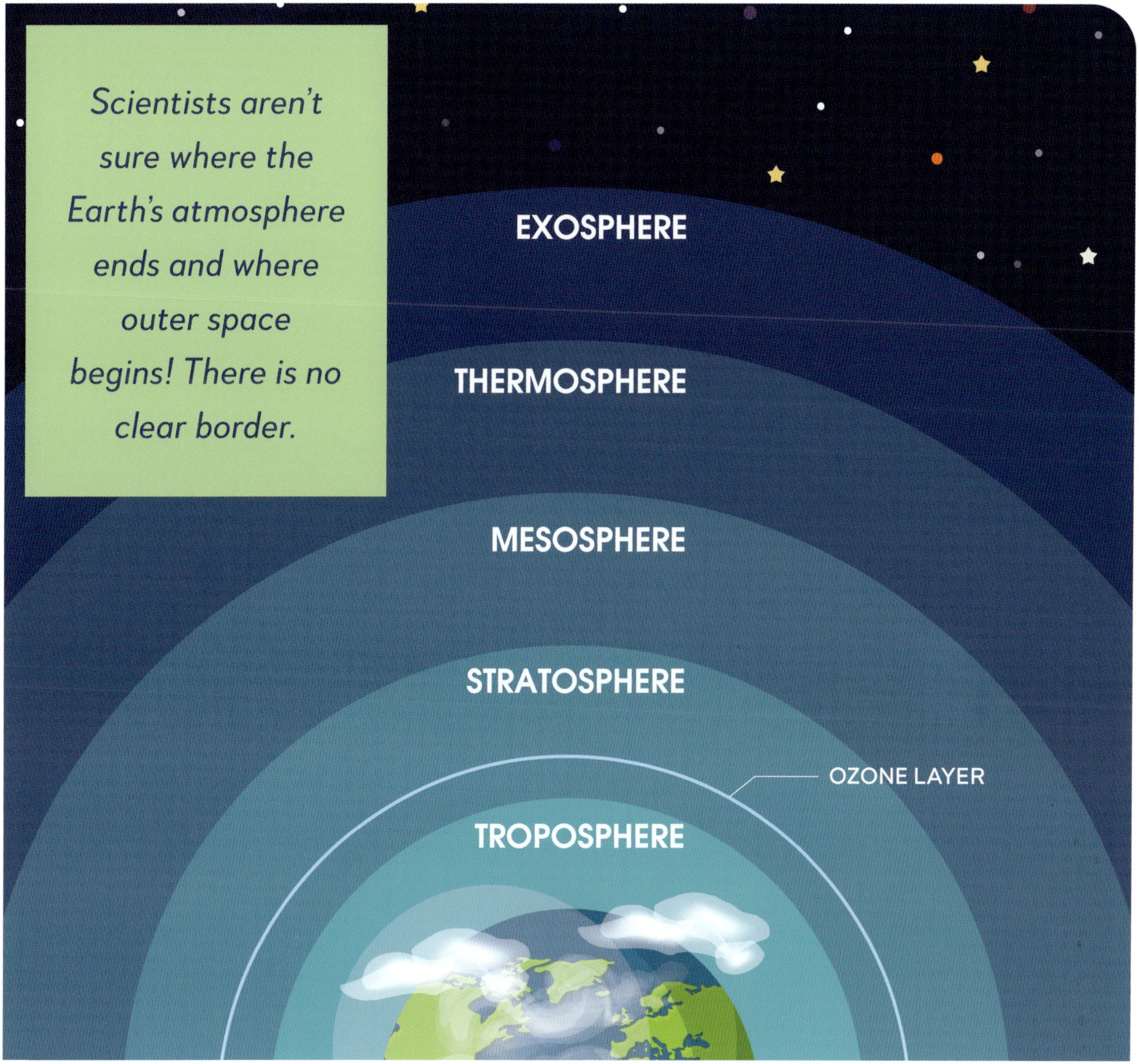

The Earth's atmosphere is important in many ways. It holds in warmth from the sun. It keeps the days from getting too hot and the nights from getting too cold. It is where **weather** like rain or snow happens.

The atmosphere also helps protect Earth from flying rocks in space called **meteoroids**. The atmosphere forces meteoroids to slow down. This makes them become hot and burn up, and stops many of them from falling to Earth.

The Ozone Layer

In the stratosphere, there is a layer called the **ozone layer**. The ozone layer helps protect animals, plants, and other living beings from the sun.

The sun is very hot and has strong rays. The ozone layer helps block these harmful rays. Without it, the sun would hurt people's skin and eyes.

In the past, people used lots of unsafe chemicals that created a large hole in the ozone layer. Today, the hole is smaller because people are using less of those chemicals.

The Earth's Orbit

Have you ever wondered where the sun goes at night?

You can't feel it, but Earth is always spinning. When one side of Earth faces the sun, it is daytime in that area. When that same side faces away, it is night. Earth makes one full turn every day.

It takes 365 days, or one year, for Earth to orbit around the sun. That's how long it takes for you to go from one birthday to your next!

An **orbit** is the journey one object in space takes around another. Earth orbits around the sun in a flattened, circle-like path.

As it orbits, Earth leans, or tilts, on its side. For part of the year, a place may face the sun and warm up. Later, that same place will face away from the sun and get colder. This is how we get our different seasons: spring, summer, fall, and winter.

The Moon

At night, you can see another large object in the sky: the moon!

The moon looks different at different times. Some nights it looks like a full circle. Other nights it looks like part of a circle. Sometimes it can't be seen at all! How can the moon change shape?

The moon's orbit is much shorter than the Earth's. It orbits Earth more than 13 times in the same amount of time it takes Earth to orbit around the sun just once.

The sun and moon are much farther from the Earth than shown here.

The moon doesn't change shape. What we see is light from the sun. How much light we see changes as the moon orbits around Earth.

When the moon is between Earth and the sun, we can't see the part of the moon that is lit up. But as it orbits, different parts light up. This creates the different moon shapes we see in the sky.

Tides

Gravity is an invisible force that pulls objects closer together.

Gravity from the moon pulls at the Earth's oceans. This pull creates long waves in the ocean, called **tides**. As the waves reach the shore, it looks like the water is slowly moving in or out. This is called high tide and low tide. High tide is when the water covers much of the shore. Low tide is when the water is farther out, and you can see more of the shore.

Gravity from the sun also helps create the tides. But the moon is much closer to Earth, so it has a stronger impact.

Some places on Earth have the same hot or cold climate for most of the year. This is due to how sunlight reaches those places.

Climate

How hot, cold, rainy, snowy, dry, and windy a place is over a long time is called **climate**.

Earth spins every day and always in the same direction. The top and bottom of Earth always face away from the sun. These areas have cold climates.

Humans have put extra carbon dioxide in the air through their use of factories, cars, and planes. Adding more carbon dioxide to the atmosphere makes it warmer. This is changing climates and affecting our world.

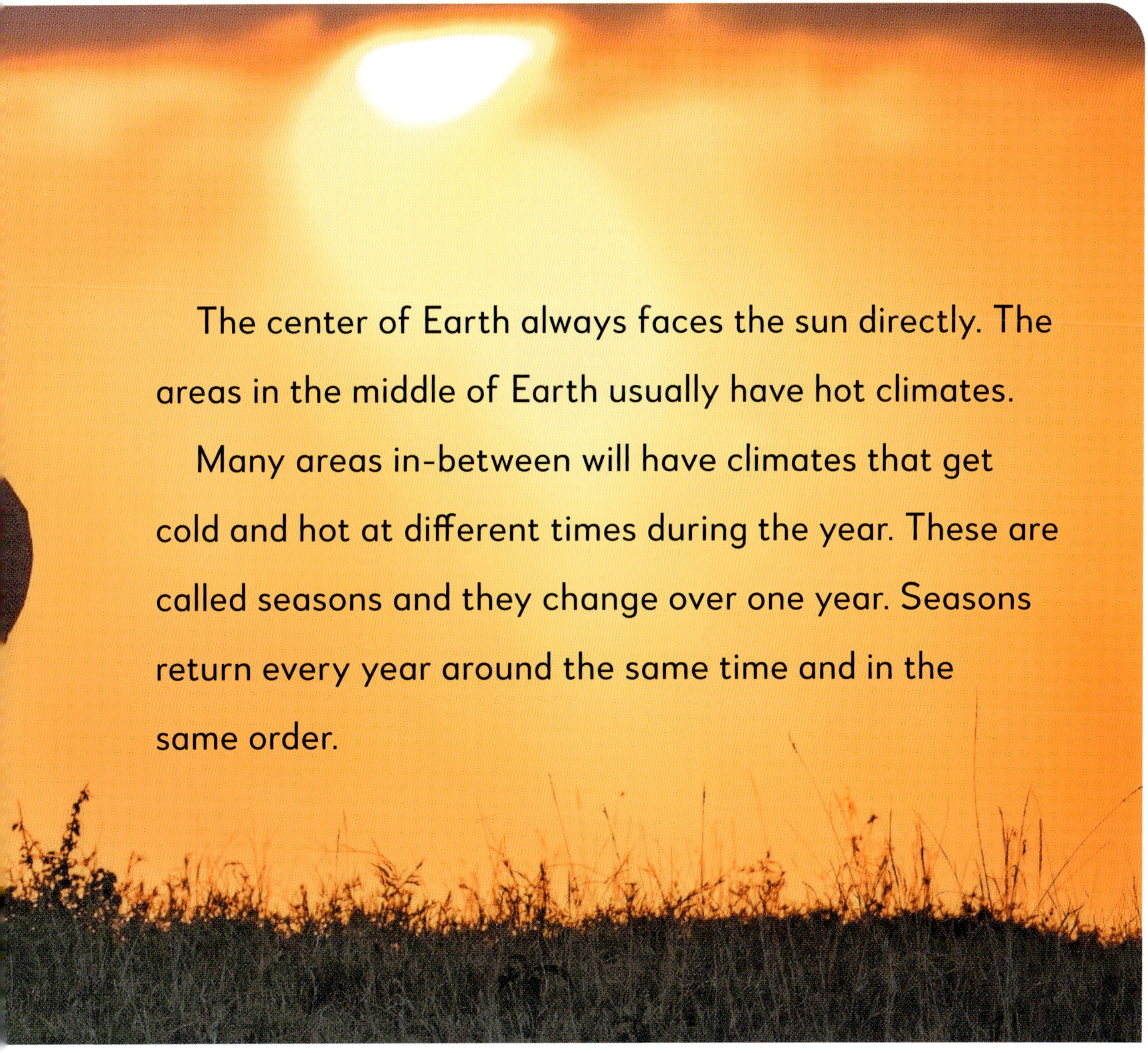

The center of Earth always faces the sun directly. The areas in the middle of Earth usually have hot climates.

Many areas in-between will have climates that get cold and hot at different times during the year. These are called seasons and they change over one year. Seasons return every year around the same time and in the same order.

Scientists use many tools to tell what the weather will be. They use computers, balloons—and they even send robots into space!

Weather

Weather is what it feels and looks like in the atmosphere outside.

Weather includes rain, snow, clouds, wind, heat, and cold. Weather is different from climate because it happens in a short time. The weather can change in just minutes. It can be sunny one moment and rainy the next!

How Heat Makes Weather

As the sun heats Earth, the atmosphere keeps some heat in. Air is warmest around the center of Earth because it gets more direct sunlight.

Air does not stay in one place. It moves around. When air moves, it also moves some of the heat. This is one way weather changes.

The oceans take in and hold more heat than land. Oceans release heat over long periods of time and keep Earth from becoming too cold.

Did you know that the air around you has weight? Even though you can't feel it, air pushes on everything it touches.

How Air Pressure Makes Weather

When gravity pushes on air, it makes **air pressure**. Air pressure can change the weather.

Warm air is lighter and rises above colder air. This causes low air pressure. Low pressure weather usually has clouds and rain.

When warm air cools, it falls and causes high air pressure. This makes weather that is dry and clear.

How Moisture Makes Weather

Air and objects can hold on to tiny amounts of water called **moisture**.

Most moisture in the air comes from the oceans. The sun heats ocean water and small amounts of water rise into the air. When the air holds a lot of water, rain or snow will fall.

Cold and hot air hold different amounts of moisture. Colder air holds less moisture, and warmer air holds more.

Have you ever walked through fog?
Then you've walked through a cloud!
Fog is a cloud that touches the ground.

Clouds

There are small things in the air we can't see, like dust. Dust gives a place for **water vapor** to hold on to, creating a small drop of water or ice crystal. Many drops or crystals together make clouds.

Clouds can be all different shapes, sizes, and colors. Look up at the clouds in the sky. What do they look like to you?

Earth and You

Earth takes care of us, so we must thank Earth by taking care of it. We can help by picking up trash, using less water, buying fewer things, and planting trees.

How can you say "thank you" to Earth today?

GLOSSARY

AIR PRESSURE: The force on a surface by air

ATMOSPHERE: The layer of gases that surrounds Earth

CLIMATE: The average weather of an area over many years

CLOUD: A group of water drops or ice crystals close together in the atmosphere

CRUST: The top layer of Earth made of rock

FRESHWATER: Water with little salt found in places like rivers, lakes, and streams

GAS: Something with no shape that will fill up a container

GRAVITY: An invisible force that pulls objects closer together

INNER CORE: The deepest layer of Earth made mostly of solid iron and nickel

LAVA: Very hot liquid rock that comes up to the Earth's surface through an opening in a volcano

LIQUID: Something that flows freely and takes the shape of a container

MAGMA: Very hot liquid and melted rock beneath the Earth's crust

MANTLE: The heavy layer under the Earth's crust made of solid and melted rock

METEOROID: A rock in outer space that orbits around the sun and is smaller than a planet

MOISTURE: Very small amounts of a liquid

MOON: An object that orbits a planet

ORBIT: A path of one object in space around another, like how the Earth orbits the sun

OUTER CORE: The layer surrounding the inner core of Earth made mostly of liquid nickel and iron

OZONE LAYER: A part of the Earth's atmosphere that helps protect living things from the harmful parts of the sun

PHOTOSYNTHESIS: The process plants use to turn sunlight, water, and carbon dioxide into energy

PLANETS: Large objects in space that move around the sun

PLATE: Large piece of the Earth's crust and upper mantle

PLATE TECTONICS: The process of large pieces of the Earth's surface moving slowly over time and making landforms

SALTWATER: Water with a lot of salt found mostly in the oceans

SOLAR SYSTEM: The sun and everything that goes around it: the eight planets and their moons and smaller objects made of rock, dust, and ice

SOLID: Something firm and stable in shape

TIDES: Long waves that move through the ocean due the moon and sun's pull from gravity

VOLCANO: An opening in the Earth's crust where lava, ash, and gases come out

WATER VAPOR: Water in the form of a gas

WEATHER: What the air and atmosphere are like at a specific time and place, such as hot, cold, windy, snowy, and rainy

ABOUT THE AUTHOR

Stephanie Manka Schuttler, PhD is a biologist, author, entrepreneur, and science communicator. Her research has taken her across the globe to study a variety of species, from flour beetles to forest elephants. She founded and runs the Fancy Scientist, LLC, where she mentors aspiring wildlife biologists and educates people on the science and conservation of wildlife.